DATE DUE

FEB 2 6 1998	
OCT 0 6 1998	
OCT 0 4 1999	

D1361375

THE ART OF AMERICA'S
SOUTHWEST
INDIANS

THE ART OF AMERICA'S
SOUTHWEST
INDIANS

GARY ALLEN HOOD

BISON GROUP

First published in 1995 by
Bison Books Ltd
Kimbolton House
117A Fulham Road
London SW3 6RL

FRED L. MATHEWS LIBRARY
58900 CHERRY GROVE RD.
DOWAGIAC, MI 49047-9726

Copyright © 1995 Bison Books Ltd

All rights reserved. No part of this publication may be reproduced,
stored in a retrieval system or transmitted in any form by any means,
electronic, mechanical, photocopying or otherwise, without first
obtaining the written permission of the copyright owner.

ISBN 1-85841-169-6

Printed in the Czech Republic

PAGE I:
**Hopi Indian Wearing
Kachina Mask**
Photograph by Kenji Kawano

PREVIOUS PAGES:
Zuni Artifacts
*American Museum of Natural
History, New York, NY
Photograph by Don Eiler*

THESE PAGES:
Hopi Wedding Manta,
c. 1910
60 × 48 inches
*Christopher Selser, Santa Fe, NM
Photograph by Herb Lotz, Santa Fe,
NM*

CONTENTS

INTRODUCTION

There is a great degree of diversity and sophistication in the arts of the American Indian. This diversification varies from architectural design and construction to aesthetic considerations in the decoration of material goods, painting, sculpture and a wide range of other products. The Indian arts of the Southwest became one of the best known among the Indian cultures because of the nature of the land in which they lived. The arid nature of the region preserved materials that can be dated back over 12,000 years of history. The Indian cultures which developed in the Southwest region of the United States are as different as the climate and landscape, varying from arid desert to fertile valleys and cool mountains.

American Indian artisans knew and respected the resources of nature and used an endless variety of natural materials in their artistic production. Each distinctive art work reflected the ideas, the concepts, and the knowledge acquired by the artist as a member of the culture in which the art was formed and for whom it was made.

The diversity of the topography and climate of the American Southwest is reflected in the multiplicity of the indigenous people that occupy it. It is a land of not only desert sand, rock and cactus but also of forests, grasslands, mountains, plateaus, fertile valleys, clear streams, lakes and wide rivers. Winters vary from cool to mild and summers from hot to warm to cool. The natural resources enjoyed by the people are incorporated into a variety of art forms. Their art developed over the course of several hundreds to even thousands of years.

The Southwest cultures developed into at least four major divisions. The oldest is the Anasazi/Basketmaker/Cliff-dweller/Pueblo group centered in two distinct areas: the Four Corners region and along the Rio Grande Valley of New Mexico. To the south in Arizona is the Hohokam-Mogollon, ancestors of the Pima and Papago. Another are the Athapascan people who came south from the far Northwest. Their descendants are the Apache and the Navajo (Dine'). The last is a mixed group of people descended from small nomadic bands that traveled throughout the areas which now comprise Arizona. Other than the Navajo and the Apache, some descended into and became known as the Chemehuevi, Havasupai, Hualapai, Mohave, Paiute, Ute, Yuma and others. All these groups settled in the Southwest and developed remarkably individual aesthetic expressions.

The first people of the Southwest hunted game and grew corn, squash and beans on the mesa tops. From about 6,000 B.C., they lived in the natural caves common to the region, and domesticated dogs and turkeys. These people were the Anasazi, "the ancient ones." By 100 B.C., their

LEFT: A full-size replica of a pithouse built by the Anasazi probably between A.D. 860 and 910 is displayed at the Anasazi Heritage Center Museum in Dolores, Colorado. Pithouses were dug into the native soil, then given finished walls and a timbered roof and furnished with features such as central hearths, partitions and storage cisterns. Families that shared these structures lived part of the time in adjacent surface apartments and used the pithouse for tasks such as food processing, tool manufacturing and rituals. (*Jackie Linder/New England Stock Photo*)

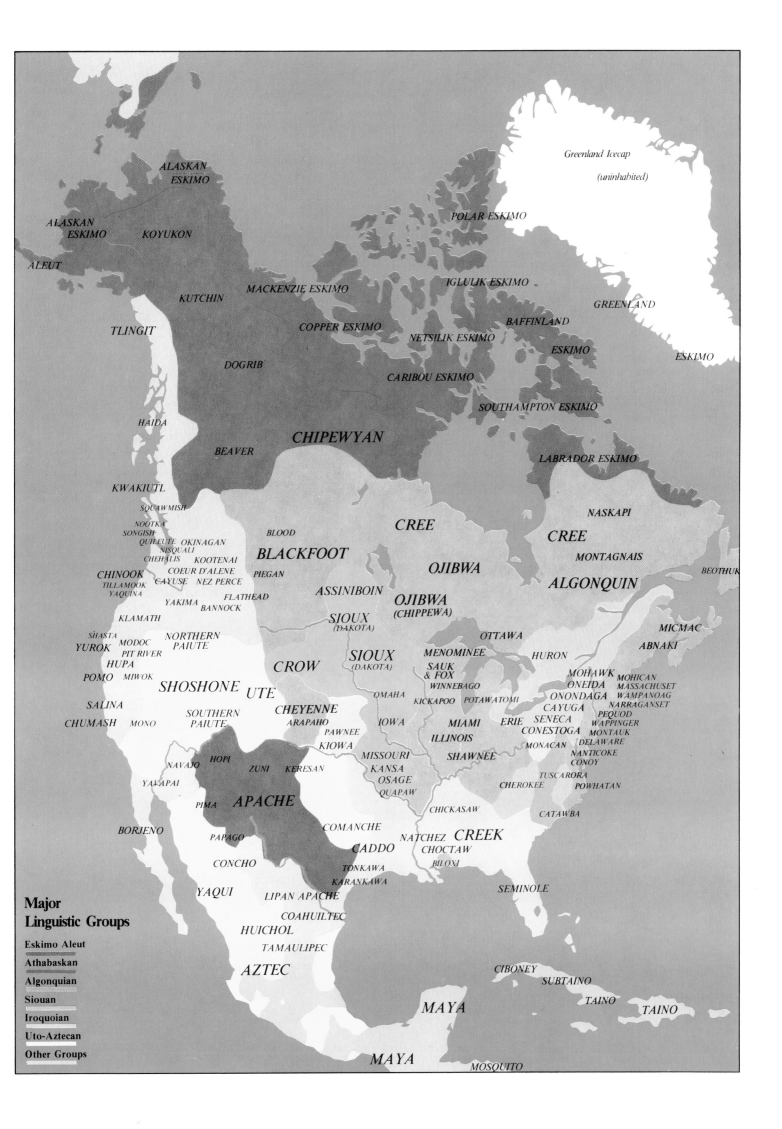

Greenland Icecap

(uninhabited)

ALASKAN
ESKIMO

POLAR ESKIMO

ALASKAN
ESKIMO   KOYUKON

ALEUT

KUTCHIN   MACKENZIE ESKIMO   IGLULIK ESKIMO

GREENLAND

COPPER ESKIMO   BAFFINLAND

TLINGIT   NETSILIK ESKIMO   ESKIMO   ESKIMO

DOGRIB   CARIBOU ESKIMO

SOUTHAMPTON ESKIMO

HAIDA

CHIPEWYAN   LABRADOR ESKIMO

BEAVER

KWAKIUTL   NASKAPI

SQUAWMISH   CREE   CREE

NOOTKA   BLOOD   MONTAGNAIS

SONGISH

QUILEUTE OKINAGAN   BLACKFOOT   OJIBWA   ALGONQUIN   BEOTHUK

NISQUALI

CHEHALIS   KOOTENAI

CHINOOK   COEUR D'ALENE   PIEGAN   OJIBWA   MICMAC

TILLAMOOK CAYUSE NEZ PERCE   (CHIPPEWA)

YAQUINA   ASSINIBOIN   ABNAKI

YAKIMA   FLATHEAD   OTTAWA

BANNOCK   SIOUX   HURON

KLAMATH   (DAKOTA)

SHASTA   MENOMINEE   MOHAWK

YUROK   MODOC   NORTHERN   CROW   SIOUX   SAUK   MOHICAN

PIT RIVER   PAIUTE   (DAKOTA)   & FOX   ONEIDA   MASSACHUSET

HUPA   WINNEBAGO   ONONDAGA   WAMPANOAG

POMO   MIWOK   OMAHA   CAYUGA   NARRAGANSET

SHOSHONE   UTE   KICKAPOO POTAWATOMI   SENECA   PEQUOD

SALINA   CHEYENNE   CONESTOGA   WAPPINGER

SOUTHERN   ARAPAHO   IOWA   MIAMI   ERIE   MONTAUK

CHUMASH   MONO   PAIUTE   PAWNEE   ILLINOIS   MONACAN   DELAWARE

KIOWA   NANTICOKE

NAVAJO   HOPI   MISSOURI   SHAWNEE   TUSCARORA   CONOY

YAVAPAI   ZUNI   KERESAN   KANSA   POWHATAN

OSAGE   CHEROKEE

PIMA   APACHE   QUAPAW

CATAWBA

BORJENO   COMANCHE

PAPAGO   NATCHEZ   CREEK

CONCHO   CADDO   CHOCTAW

TONKAWA   BILOXI

YAQUI   KARANKAWA   SEMINOLE

LIPAN APACHE

COAHUILTEC

HUICHOL

TAMAULIPEC

AZTEC   CIBONEY

SUBTAINO

MAYA   TAINO   TAINO

MAYA

MOSQUITO

**Major
Linguistic Groups**

Eskimo Aleut

Athabaskan

Algonquian

Siouan

Iroquoian

Uto-Aztecan

Other Groups

LEFT: The White House Ruins at Canyon de Chelly, Arizona, photographed by Ben Wittick in 1903. The Anasazi, or "ancient ones," often selected dwelling sites in the sandstone cliffs that would be difficult for enemies to access and were near running water. The adobe structures built into the cliff face at Canyon de Chelly were probably constructed between A.D. 1100 and 1200. (*The Museum of New Mexico*)

lifestyle developed into one commonly called the Basketmaker culture. The remnants of many of their baskets have been found in caves, but there is no record of permanent housing for these people. They made baskets for every purpose, even for cooking, and wove blankets and made jewelry from natural materials.

Pithouses were made by the descendants of the Basketmakers. Three of them were excavated in 1926 at Step House Cave in Mesa Verde (Spanish words meaning "green table"), Colorado. Pithouse structures are made with supports of upright poles interwoven with branches and faced with adobe, a sunbaked clay mixed with straw. By the end of the Basketmaker period, A.D. 700, hundreds of these pithouse villages were constructed on the mesas, and clay replaced basketry for use as utilitarian vessels as well as for architectural building blocks.

Around A.D. 750, Basketmaker culture evolved into the Pueblo, a Spanish word meaning village. Architectural structures became more "communal" as pithouses were joined end to end in long curving rolls, almost always facing south. The new pueblo structures are built above ground using advanced masonry techniques to make vertical adobe brick walls. However, the old pithouse tradition was preserved with the underground ceremonial rooms called kivas, which were now roofed almost flush with the ground. They are metaphors for the underworld, from whence all things come into the world.

The most impressive building of the Great Pueblo period is the crescent-shaped four-storied structure called Pueblo Bonito in Chaco Canyon, New Mexico. It was built and occupied around A.D. 900, and by the time it was finished about 1100, it had 650 rooms and a number of underground kivas of various sizes in the great forecourt. It was abandoned by 1150 when the residents may have been driven out by drought or marauders. It was built on a valley floor at the base of the mesa. At Pueblo Bonito, the outer ring of rooms originally rose four stories, with hundreds of sleeping rooms facing the court and storerooms lining the back.

At Mesa Verde, around the year 1200, this general ordering of spaces, as evident in Pueblo Bonito, was followed when the Pueblo apparently yielded to hostile pressure and moved from the mesa tops and the shadow of the mesas to the large caves and chambers on mesa cliff faces. The builders of the adobe structures on the cliff sides improvised around the natural terrain of each recessed area selected as a dwelling place.

The dwelling places were carefully selected so the winter's rising sun would warm them in the morning and the rock would retain some heat through the day. In the summer, however, proper site selection also made cool evenings the norm. Natural springs or streams were often located at the base of the cliffs. The cliff sites were also selected for their inaccessibility. They could only be entered by holds cut into the cliff faces or by removable ladders. They did not regularize the natural forms to fit their needs; rather, they let the natural terrain determine the structure of their buildings. Nevertheless, at Cliff Palace in Mesa Verde the Pueblo were able to build over 200 rooms and excavate more than 20 ceremonial kiva chambers. Also constructed during the 1200's were Balcony House, Spruce Tree House, and Square Tower House.

Cliff villages were not laid out in advance. Instead, they gradually assumed their final forms as new buildings defined various court areas. Mesa Verde's Spruce Tree House is an excellent example of classic Pueblo architecture: shaped masonry, pole supported floors and balconies, retaining walls, smoothly engineered courts, and towers rising the meet the cave ceiling. Small niches in the back of the major structures served for grain storage. The two- and three-story apartments were used primarily as sleeping rooms which could be entered through keyshaped doorways. These types of door openings were also common at the Chaco Canyon structures.

Most unique to Pueblo village life was the round kiva, basically a male dominated religious and ceremonial subterranean chamber with an adobe covered wooden ceiling supported from the inside by stone or wood piers. The participants entered through a central hatch and probably sat on masonry benches set up between the interior supports. Air for the underground room entered through an L-shaped vent shaft. A stone slab, set up in front the vent's opening into the room, deflected the air which then rose with smoke from the fire in the center of the room, to escape through the hatchway. On axis with the firepit and vent was a hole called the "sipapu" which symbolized an opening into the spirit world.

Classic Pueblo culture declined in the fifteenth century; cliff life had died out around 1300. This decline and abandonment was initially caused by a long drought period that lasted some twenty years between 1276 and 1299 as determined by tree-ring dating. Also, there is much speculation that the people were harassed by nomadic tribes, probably the ancestors of the Navajo, Athapascans who had drifted down from central Canada.

Modern Pueblos retain some of the same structure types using the old building methods with similar materials. For example, the longest occupied location in North America is Acoma Pueblo in west central New Mexico. Acoma's one- and two-storied structures are aligned loosely in avenues, just as they must have been during the Great Pueblo period eleven centuries ago. While Pueblo Acoma

ABOVE: The magnificent
Cliff Palace at Mesa Verde
National Park in Colorado
contained more than 200
rooms. (*Margo Taussig
Pinkerton/New England
Stock Photo*)

OPPOSITE: An aerial view of
Pueblo Bonito at the Chaco
Culture National Historic
Park in New Mexico. The
outer ring of some 650
rooms originally rose four
stories. It was probably
built between A.D. 900 and
1100. (*R. Perron/New
England Stock Photo*)

RIGHT: The ancient method
of building multi-story
adobe structures was
carried on by many of the
Southwestern tribes. This
photograph of the Hopi
Dance Rock at Walpi
Pueblo, Arizona, was taken
by John K. Hillers in 1879.
(*Smithsonian Institution*)

is a good example of the structures of the Great Pueblo period, survival of the classic Pueblo architectural form as evidenced by Pueblo Bonito, of eight centuries past, is seen at Taos Pueblo in New Mexico. This example is, of course, the classic ordering and stacking of cubic masses. The round kiva also still survives in the Southwest as a ceremonial structure.

The structure of Navajo hogans possesses some of the components of Pueblo kivas. The modern hogan is built of split rails, or actual railroad ties, and sometimes is heaped with earth around the outside. The hogan has the round plan and corbeled roof that harkens back to the pithouses of the Southwest's early inhabitants.

The Hohokam is named after a Pima Indian word meaning "those who have gone." The culture was centered in southern Arizona and can be traced to at least 300 B.C., probably originally indigenous to Mexico. By 1450, Hohokam largely abandoned the region due to incursions of more people into the Southwest and changes in the climate. However, Papago and Pima Indians are considered their descendants. During their thousand years in the Southwest, the Hohokam developed a high degree of achievement in their art forms, most in pottery and jewelry made of trade shells. Casa Grande National Monument and Pueblo Grande, both in southern Arizona, are the remnants of their villages.

The Mogollon culture of farmers and pottery makers dates from about 300 B.C. to A.D. 1500. It is named after a mountain range in southern Arizona and New Mexico. In their early traditions and lifestyle, they were related to the Anasazi. Although they built pithouses, the Mogollon did

BELOW: This deep gray bowl with zigzag motif was made by the Anasazi between A.D. 500 and 700 near La Plata River, Colorado. (*J. Beckett and A. Anik/American Museum of Natural History, New York, NY*)

ABOVE: Acoma Pueblo is the longest continually occupied location in North America. The one- and two-storied adobe buildings are built along avenues, similar to Anasazi villages. (*Ansel Adams/National Archives*)

LEFT: This old-style Navajo hogan has much in common with Anasazi pithouses. (*Kenji Kawano*)

not as fully abandon hunting and gathering in favor of more permanent dwellings. They did not widely practice irrigation methods because they lived in the higher elevations where more rainfall was common. Their distinctive red-on-brown pottery is the earliest known in the Southwest.

The Southwestern antecedents of the Pueblo people expressed themselves along established and accepted cultural patterns forged over a long period of time. They created a language of symbols which structured their art within a wide variety of intricate design and theme combinations. Bold experimentation was conducted within these guidelines. Despite conventions, Pueblo artists were able to create imaginative, free-flowing artistic impressions. Firm control of linear elements and a high degree of technical competence are characteristic of the art of the region. Southwest Indians mastered involved design concepts.

Living slightly to the east of the Hohokam were the early Mimbres people (1000 to 1150), who produced unique linear patters and some naturalistic designs and figurative paintings on their pottery forms. However, because of their lack of high quality clay, they could not produce the elegant pottery forms of their distant neighbors. Their intricate designs, however, are delicate inscriptions in black

on a white ground. The drawings abound with drama, humor and sharp observation. They are full of vigorous life, animation and activity. The development of their unique pottery art style may be due, at least in part, to their relative isolation in contrast to the practically urban setting in which the Anasazi lived.

The Athapascans were the forerunners of the Navajo and the Apache. Arriving in the Southwest around 1300 A.D., they introduced a few new concepts. But theirs was more a story of cultural adaptation. Having traveled over a period of many years from the area of northwestern Canada to the more temperate climate of the Southwest, the Athapascans brought little with them. After arriving in the region, they quickly made accommodations in their culture and lifestyle to adapt to their new homeland.

There is some evidence to suggest that the Athapascans made belts and matting with grasses and fibers. Apparently, the Athapascans learned weaving with the loom from the early Pueblo people. Cotton was replaced by wool after its introduction by the Spaniards who originally arrived in the Southwest in 1520. The Navajo, descendants of the Athapascans, dominate the field of American Indian textiles.

Among the neighboring tribes of the Navajo were the Mohave, Yuma and Ute. In pottery and, particularly, in basketry, they developed a distinctive combination of forms, designs and identifiable styles.

Because of the preservation qualities of the dry climate, more is known of the historical development of the cultures of the Southwest peoples than of any other area in North America. Most of the earliest examples of reliable data on human occupation in the Americas have been found in the region. Cliff houses and dry caves protected perishable materials such as basketry, pottery, textiles, and carved wood. Tree-ring and radio carbon dating allow scientists to accurately prescribe specific dates to certain sites. The techniques used in dating archeological sites also allows for the establishment of relationships between inhabitants of far-flung sites. Through this, an understanding can be achieved of the cultural relativism of the early peoples and their descendants who still live in the region.

Indians of all regions were active traders, accounting for the reason that many Indian art forms and material products were also known and produced far from their places of origin. Indian traders, and later the white traders, used ancient trade routes extending from the Atlantic to the Pacific and from the Gulf Coast to the interior of Canada.

OPPOSITE: A Navajo weaver, Mrs. Alice Longhorse derives her main income from the weavings she makes in her studio at her hogan in Fort Defiance, Arizona. Mrs. Longhorse has taught her daughters and granddaughters the traditional art of weaving. (*Kenji Kawano*)

RIGHT: This nineteenth-century photograph of a Navajo woman at a horizontal loom was taken by Timothy O'Sullivan. (*UPI/Bettmann*)

BELOW: This prehistoric cotton robe was found wrapped around a mummy in a cave in Grand Gulch, Utah. The design on this extremely rare piece is similar to designs on textiles from the historic period. (*J. Cox and P. Goldberg/ American Museum of Natural History, New York, NY*)

The art of the Plains and the Southwest are especially good examples of this active trade. Shells were traded for such items as pipestone and turquoise, weaving was exchanged for buckskin, and feathers were bartered for foods or paint pigments. In traveling these long distances, traders absorbed other ideas about form and design and exchanged concepts as well as materials. The designs were sometimes altered and improved by local craftsmen.

Members of each tribe use certain techniques and create particular styles as a result of their traditions. No two blankets, no two baskets and no two kachina dolls are exactly alike. However, many tribes traded ideas among themselves and adapted the things learned into their own traditions and methods of making objects.

Elaborately ornamented bags and pouches were used to carry food and tobacco and to protect such valued possessions as pipes and guns. They were constructed of hide, fibers of grass or reed, cotton or wool yarn or string. Pipe bags ornamented with bead and quillwork were traditionally important in Plains culture. Some could be found in the Southwest. Bags used by the Southwest Indian people were woven on looms. Similar bags used by the Eastern Woodland Indians were woven by hand.

Cradleboards appear throughout North American Indian cultures. The Pima of the Southwest made ladder-like constructions of wood to which the baby was held with cloth or hide bindings. The portable baby carriers provided an infant with a warm and secure environment. They could be suspended from trees or carried on the mother's back.

Among the Indians of the Southwest, an example of the decoration of functional objects is seen on the large quantity of ancient pottery objects which have survived. Although the clay vessels themselves may not be remarkable in themselves, the sharply painted patterns on many of the objects reveal uncommon skill.

Ancient Southwestern art (often called "prehistoric" because it was made prior to the arrive of Europeans) is mostly linear in design. That is, the artist preferred to decorate by inscribing lines on the surface of the object. However, instead of being realistically rendered with recognizable symbols, most of the patters were abstract and often geometric in design. There was social and spiritual stricture against realistically rendered pictures. The earliest pottery and basketry were sparsely decorated. Later pottery became more decorative. Scholars call it black-on-

LEFT: Cradleboards were used by Southwestern women to carry their babies on their backs while they went about their daily tasks. These two Apache babies bundled up in their cradles were photographed before 1884. (*Phoebe Hearst Museum of Anthropology, University of California, Berkeley*)

ABOVE: Anasazi pottery, dated from A.D. 1100, found in Pueblo Bonito, Chaco Canyon, New Mexico. Thongs were probably strung through the loops near the tops of the vessels to facilitate carrying water. Note the similarity of the designs to those found on later Pueblo pottery. (*P. Hollembeak/American Museum of Natural History, New York, NY*)

LEFT: Hopi women decorating pottery, in a 1903 photograph by Underwood and Underwood. The two young girls wear the traditional hairstyle for unmarried women. (*Reproduced from the collections of the Library of Congress*)

white pottery because of the black lines painted on white forms. The "Golden Age" of ancient Pueblo pottery took place about 1000 to 1400. Ceremonial figures were portrayed and abstract symbols seemed to be inserted for specific purposes related to social and religious harmony. At this important time in the development of Pueblo arts, the cities of the early historic period also began to thrive – Awatovi, Kuaua, Pottery Mound, Pueblo Bonito and others. In addition to the large number of pottery works found at these sites, murals have been excavated. They reveal the previously unsuspected importance of image and design in the painting and ceremonials of early Pueblo people.

Based on traditions developed over several thousand years, Pueblo art in particular is a continuum of ancient concepts, designs, techniques and forms. The continuum of cultural development has also been effected successively by the development of new art forms and tools by which to produce art. Therefore, striking parallels may be made that mark relationships between modern art forms by Indian artists and ancient symbols, designs and forms.

However, despite the signs of cultural continuum, there was not and is not one art that is common to all people throughout the Southwest. Quite the contrary is true, because of the diversity of the heritage of peoples that occupy the region. The conventional geometric forms of the Anasazi, the Pueblo forebears, are in stark contrast to the more fanciful designs of the Hohokam people who were the ancestors of the Pima and Papago.

Pottery has been the most enduring of the art forms of the tribes of the Southwest, which includes the states of New Mexico and Arizona. Since so-called prehistoric times, Indian crafts people have produced a variety of clay pottery forms. Although most pottery was made for cooking or storage, it was nevertheless decorated with painted or etched designs. All pottery was made from clay and generally by the method known as coiling, in which coils of clay were spiraled around until the desired size and shape were formed.

After digging the clay from a natural deposit such as a river bank, the potter removed the pebbles and crushed and ground it into a fine powder, often using a mano and metate (mortar and pestle). A finely crushed tempering material of limestone, sand, shell, or plant fibers was added to the clay to prevent it from cracking during drying and firing. The final step to ready clay for use was to add water and knead the wet clay on a flat surface until it became the consistency of putty.

The potter prepared the clay coils by rolling them between the hands. A flat pancake of clay was made for the bottom of the pot. The coil was laid around the rim of the pancake, and coils were continually added one above the other while the potter squeezed them between her fingers until they reached the desired thickness and the correct inward or outward slope. After the pot had dried in the sun, the outside of the pot was wetted and smoothed with a scraper. The pot was then decorated with a creamy mixture of colored clay called slip (white, yellow, tan, or red). Finally, the pot was placed in, over or under a fire to make it hard.

Each Southwest tribe used certain shapes and designs for their pots, and the pottery of each region can be recognized and identified from these shapes and designs. The painting of the pottery in the Southwest varied from the

LEFT: Two Zuni women carry water jars, or ollas, on their heads in this 1903 Edward Curtis photograph. Note the kilns, used for baking pottery, in the background. (*Reproduced from the collections of the Library of Congress*)

OPPOSITE: The Pottery Dance, performed today by Zuni women, recalls the days when young women carried water from a spring to the village in pots balanced gracefully on their heads. (*Kenji Kawano*)

LEFT: An Apache bride, bedecked in finery and holding a basket probably made either by herself or her mother, in a late nineteenth century photograph. (*National Archives*)

OPPOSITE: Edward Curtis's photograph entitled *Navajo Still Life* was probably taken around 1903. (*Special Collections Division, University of Washington Libraries*)

fanciful designs of the Pima and Papago to the conventionalized geometric forms of the Pueblo people. Thus, the early Pueblo people developed a more rigid form of design that the free-flowing concepts of artistic design found further west. Nevertheless, all were masters of involved and endless variations in design concepts based on traditional themes.

Hopi pottery is painted in various shades of orange and red. The designs are based on ancient elements drawn from nature. Zuni pottery designs are made as primarily black decoration applied to a pot before it is fired. The pottery bases are painted with a black or brown colored slip. The rest of the vessel is divided into horizontally zoned sections with stepped, geometric forms, rosettes, arches and animals such as birds and deer. The Zuni also commonly make bowls with stepped rims decorated with naturalistic animal forms.

Pueblo pottery can be distinguished for the most part by the characteristic styles common to each Pueblo. For example, Acoma Pueblo produces thin pottery with all-over geometric designs as well as bird and flower patterns. Modern Acoma ware is characterized by fine geometric patterns in black on white similar to prehistoric examples. Polished red and black pottery is common to the Santa Clara Pueblo, which is sometimes decorated with impressed designs. Maria Martinez made the pottery of San Ildefonso Pueblo famous. In the early 1900s, she revived many of the traditional designs and techniques in her exquisite black ware with geometric matte designs on shiny surfaces.

Along the lower Colorado River region in Arizona, the Yuma and Mohave tribes made pottery dolls decorated with beads and sometimes with cloth. Originally conceived as toys or for religious purposes, now varied forms are made for sale. Designs and styles have been altered or elaborated upon and adapted to the demand for sales. For example, in pottery and basketry surface decoration now predominates over the previous storage function of the container. The arts of weaving and silversmithing are also in demand. Southwest Indian art of the present is essen-

tially a continuum of earlier prehistoric forms and techniques, effected by the introduction of new tools and materials to develop methods of creating traditional shapes and designs.

Long before pottery came into use in the Southwest, about 300 B.C., and even before it was used in the Eastern Woodlands where it was developed about 2000 B.C., baskets had been used since at least 7000 B.C. Native American baskets were woven from a variety of plant materials by three basic techniques: plaiting, coiling, and twining.

Basket making was practiced all over the continent, by tribes from the Pacific to the Atlantic. In basketry and the textile arts the basic weavings were frequently embellished with appliquéd designs or embroidery. Most Southwestern art served a functional purpose. However, although much less common, designs applied to objects to make them visually attractive was not entirely unknown. Among some cultures, after a useful life, richly embellished ceremonial art might be burned, buried or otherwise ritualistically destroyed.

Coiling and twining were the techniques commonly used for basket making in the Southwest. The simplest technique is plaiting, consisting of the crisscrossing of fiber elements or alternately passing over and under the parts of another set.

The best method for making burden and pack baskets is twining, which involves firmly securing horizontal elements with vertical elements. Different colors of fibers are used to weave designs into the baskets. The weaving of intricate colorful designs on the soles of fiber sandals show the same kind of vital expression.

Coiled baskets can be identified by the rope-like coils that look like a spiral on the bottom with the sides of the basket appearing horizontal. The Hopi, Papago, and Pima most commonly use this method of basket making. Coiled baskets are made with thin strips of fibers that are wrapped in a bundle and coiled in a continuous spiral to shape the form of the basket. New coils are lashed and sewn to each previous coil.

Textiles were also produced over the various cultural areas of the North American continent. Various tribes produced cloth by the techniques of finger weaving, twining, plaiting, netting, looping, knitting, and crocheting. Loom weaving was done only in the Southwest.

Indian clothing, particularly ceremonial garments, served a social and decorative function as well as a physical one. The most widely known garments are hide garments worn by the Plains people, but designs also reached great heights among the Pueblo people.

The earliest Pueblo clothing was woven with cotton thread. However, wool came into common use after the arrival of the Spanish and the introduction of sheep. Men's clothing consisted of breechcloths, kilts, poncho-like shirts and rabbit-fur robes. Women wore a dress or manta (a cloth rectangle embroidered on the sides and tied at the waist with a sash), buckskin leggings and boot-like moccasins. For major ceremonials, women wore white cotton "wedding robes" and wool shawls embroidered with colored yarn in symbolic motifs that originated in pre-Columbian times.

Blankets were an important part of Navajo life. They were used to provide warmth, to sit on, as bedding, and as saddle blankets. Navajo women weave blankets on vertical looms, using a technique learned from the neighboring Pueblo people with whom it had been in use since about 1000 A.D. Original materials consisted of cotton colored with vegetable dyes. The Spanish introduced the use of wool and a variety of new designs. The classic geometric patterns of Navajo blankets are best exemplified by the "chief" blankets woven in the mid-nineteenth century. These passed through four design phases, from simple

OPPOSITE: The Miss Navajo Contest, held in the western part of Navajoland in early September, showcases traditional women's skills. Here a woman weaves a wedding basket, which will be at least 10 inches in diameter when completed. Blue corn mash is served in such baskets as part of the wedding celebration. (*Kenji Kawano*)

RIGHT: Two San Carlos Apaches pose for a staged photograph by A.F. Randall around 1884. (*Phoebe Hearst Museum of Anthropology, University of California, Berkeley*)

BELOW: A Hopi bride wears the traditional wedding manta in this Edward Curtis photograph. (*Reproduced from the collections of the Library of Congress*)

striped patterns through rectangular blocks set in stripes to a combination of stripes and diamonds. The introduction of aniline dyes in the 1880s enabled the Navajo weavers to use brilliant colors in the zig-zagging patterns of the vivid "eye-dazzler" blankets. During the early twentieth century the government discouraged Indian crafts, but by the time new laws were passed dealing with the production of Indian arts and crafts, complex geometric designs were becoming common. Examples are the weavings produced around Ganado and Two Gray Hills in the country of the Navajo Nation.

There is a tradition of stone art among the Southwest tribes dating back to their earliest occupation in the region, thousands of years ago. Most of this art was very small in scale. Like the Zuni fetish figures, they represented animal subjects such as wolf, bear, coyote, eagle, and cougar. Each denoted a sacred region, a spirit, or one of the natural elements.

Fetishes are small animal figures carved in stone, usually basalt. They are used as good luck charms. They were originally created by the Zuni people whose land is in west central New Mexico. Although these figures were early employed in sacred ceremonies by the Zuni, without

the ceremonial connotation many are made for commercial sale. The carvings were sometimes inlaid with turquoise or other stones to represent eyes, necklaces and lifelines. Their origins in prehistoric times suggest ancient legends of animals being turned into stone. Therefore, the pieces most highly prized were natural stones and rocks which resembled animals without being carved. The stones, either natural or carved, were believed to have indwelling spirits that gave their owners supernatural power. When not in use, they were stored in special containers and ceremoniously "fed." These small sculptures served as charms for physical health and well being.

Throughout prehistory, stone was also shaped into useful tools, such as axes, and continued to be used even into the nineteenth century, after traders had introduced metal tools and weapons. Stone was important not only for tools but also as a source for weapons and hunting implements. It was also widely used for ornaments, such as beads, pendants, and earrings. In the preparation of foods, stone was shaped into manos and metates.

As masters of the applied arts, the people of the Southwest achieved a high degree of individual art expression in a variety of styles and media. For example, they embellished the simple forms of their pottery with a wide variety of painted designs, both naturalistic and abstract. They also had a tradition of mural painting as seen in remnants remaining on kiva walls. Their culture, as seen through their arts, identify psychological, philosophical and aesthetic qualities which help scholars identify the disparate groups of people and given them each a cultural identity.

Active trade was a major component in the development of the arts of the Southwest. At the same time trade was conducted in physical materials, ideas were also interchanged about design and symbols, naturalistic forms and abstractions. For example, the Navajo not only borrowed Pueblo weaving techniques but also adapted the sand painting techniques of the Hopi and Zuni. They mastered, refined and expanded the art form to an incredibly complex series of ceremonial and other adapted designs. Sand painting is now less commonly exercised among the other tribes of the region but continues to be a major practice by the Navajo. They utilize special designs in their religious

OPPOSITE: A Navajo weaving in the Third Phase Chief's Blanket design, by Anita Harvey Tsosie, circa 1991. 72 × 75 inches, all commercial respun wool. (*Courtesy of Cristof's/ Photography by Mark Nohl*)

ABOVE RIGHT: This small frog effigy, made of jet inlaid with turquoise, was found at Pueblo Bonito. (*American Museum of Natural History, New York, NY*)

RIGHT: Many of the ancient symbols found in petroglyphs have retained their significance, and appear as design elements in various art forms. (*Kenji Kawano*)

ceremonies and Navajo artists also practice a special kind of naturalistic picture sand painting for collectors of the craft.

Within the last 150 years, Navajo weaving has become more prominent than Pueblo weaving. Whereas Pueblo weavers worked primarily for home consumption, the Navajos supplied not only their domestic needs but also made products specifically for the marketplace. The value of the market went up as more and more immigrants came into the area. As soon as the white man came into the Navajo world, he became a prime consumer of Indian-produced goods. Many Navajo women became at least part-time weavers for commercial outlets.

Silversmithing also became an important means of producing income for the Navajo people. Silverwork is one of the most widely collected crafts of the North American Indian. In the mid-nineteenth century the Navajo learned the metalwork trade from Mexican ironsmiths. They were aware of brass and copper work through their trading networks, but did not learn how to work with it until their experience with the Mexican smiths. The Navajo were imprisoned at Bosque Redondo in the Fort Sumner, New Mexico Territory, Army post between 1863 and 1868. Afterwards, they acquired silver coins from traders and

LEFT: A Navajo silversmith displays his tools and examples of his work in this circa 1880 photograph by Ben Wittick. (*National Archives*)

OPPOSITE: A Zuni woman wearing impressive turquoise jewelry holds a pot that she has made, at the Intertribal Ceremonial in Gallup, New Mexico. The gathering, which includes a pow-wow, parades and various competitions, has been held on the second weekend of August for 70 years. (*Kenji Kawano*)

began to create their first rudimentary silverwork – bracelets and earrings.

The first Navajo squash blossom necklace designs were a take-off on Mexican pomegranate designs. Navajo silversmiths also created crescents, bowguards, bracelets, buckles, powder chargers, tobacco flasks, conchas and brooches. Cutting, hammering, casting and soldering were among the techniques the Navajo learned prior to 1900. The Zuni learned silversmithing from the Navajo in the 1870s and the Hopi learned from the Zuni in the 1890s. A few other tribes in the Southwest also learned the craft. Nevertheless, the majority of Indian silversmithing and

jewelry is the accomplishment of the Navajo. Rich mineral deposits and geological resources provide the minerals that are widely used in Southwestern jewelry. The natural pigments of the minerals are also used by the Navajo and Hopi in the creation of their sand painting designs.

Southwest sculpture was primarily made of wood, and there are few known examples in stone or metal. Hopi and Pueblo kachina dolls are perhaps the best known sculptural forms in the Southwest. Kachinas are supernatural beings responsible for harmonious balance through a wide variety of religious and social activities among several of the Southwest Indian peoples. There are few duplications

LEFT: Zuni dancers perform the Eagle Dance. Sacred to all American Indians, the eagle is believed to be a messenger between the people and the sky deities. Note the large bells the dancers wear on their legs. (*Kenji Kawano*)

BELOW: Traditionally-clad Zuni dancers, some of whom wear wooden handmade tablitas on their heads, participate in a parade during the Zuni Fair, held at the end of August at Zuni Pueblo in Arizona. (*Kenji Kawano*)

among the many designs and people have developed a tremendous range of types in order to distinguish and identify them. These carved and painted figures depict kachina dancers (representing kachina spirits) who perform in ceremonies related to hunting, agriculture and the continuity of life. The dolls, carved of the root of cottonwood, a sacred tree, were originally made to teach children the pantheon of over 350 kachina characters. The artist effectively combines his wooden form with elaborate color, cloth, feather and other ornamentation in a prescribed representation of a particular kachina spirit. Kachina dolls were originally simple and small block-like figures with only traces of painted decoration. The facial mask was emphasized and the body was only secondarily considered. Eventually, the body was lengthened and the overall quality of the figure became tantamount. Forms became most realistic and detailed. Kachina carvings are now more imitative of the human form and the postures of the dancers.

Kachina spirits and personages are important to the ritual of the Southwest Pueblo tribes. The small kachina figures represent the male performers wearing painted leather or cloth masks and a beautifully decorated costume. While familiar to all Pueblo peoples, the wooden Kachina dolls have been highly developed by the Hopi and Zuni. The classic kachinas tend to be taller than more recent carvings, and older Zuni examples frequently have movable arms. The oldest examples are blocky in form, abstract in conception and were made strictly for tribal use. Kachina dolls, made for sale to tourists, have become more naturalistic and rigid earlier styles have given way to realistic dance poses and elaborately rendered detail.

In the Southwest, cylinder-shaped masks of hide, painted with geometric designs and often decorated with feathers, are worn by dancers impersonating kachinas and wooden tablitas are sometimes attached to masks depicting specific kachina spirits. Masks of painted cloth and wood are worn in the Apache Gan Dance. Many kinds of headdresses are worn in Southwestern ceremonial dances. Wood carved, terrace edged tablitas (thin, flat panels worn on top of the head) are used in Pueblo ceremonials such as the Corn Dance.

Also used in Southwest ceremonials are dance wands – flat, painted boards carried by women dancers as part of ceremonies related to agriculture and rotation of the seasons. The earliest examples are made of yucca wood, later ones of pine. Usually used in pairs, they are painted with representations of human figures and kachinas.

Ceremonials are often accompanied by musical instruments. Indian ceremonial life includes rattles, flutes, stringed instruments and drums. Rattles are made of gourds or two pieces of hollowed-out wood, partially filled with small pebbles and then tied together.

ABOVE: Pueblo dancers perform the Deer Dance at the Intertribal Ceremonial in Gallup, New Mexico. (*Kenji Kawano*)

The rawhide shield is one of the most widely dispersed object categories of Indian culture. Shields were used by nomadic hunters and warriors in the Eastern Woodlands, the Plains and the Southwest. Ornamented with strongly individualistic imagery which often incorporates birds, horses and animal tracks, shields were objects of mystical heraldry and their images were originally transmitted through visions to their owners, who later painted them on their shields. Predominantly symbolic shields were kept at the warrior's side or suspended near his dwelling so that their mystical imagery could serve as protection.

The age of specialization in Indian arts began late in the

LEFT: Pueblo children learning the Buffalo Dance in New Mexico. The elaborate costumes worn for the dances are carefully assembled by each dancer, sometimes using contemporary elements and often including items made by a member of the family. (*Bachmann/New England Stock Photo*)

OPPOSITE: Dancers at Santa Clara Pueblo perform the Corn Dance. The evergreen boughs symbolize life. (*Gail Russell*)

nineteenth century. Until the middle of the nineteenth century, most men made their own objects for everyday use, as well as for religious or ceremonial activities. By specializing in the making of a particular type of art, such as silversmithing, more could be produced as skills were honed. Thus, among their other silversmithing skills, the Navajo men practice a form of casting to produce distinctive, heavy cast silver jewelry. The Navajo women specialize in intricately designed weavings; and the Hopi weavers design the light and delicate ceremonial robes, dance sashes and belts.

For example, specialization results in the finely de-
tailed, intricate inlay work of coral, turquoise, shell and jet produced by the Zuni and neighboring Pueblos. The Rio Grande Pueblos do not produce many textiles or baskets. Their artists focus on making objects of clay. Within the specialities of the Hopi and the Apache are the production of high quality baskets.

The production of the handbuilt pottery crafted by the Pueblos has also become highly specialized. However, adaptations in designs and styles have occurred to satisfy collector demand. Skillful application of the surface decoration is still a predominant consideration, as is the shaping of the vessel. Many are intended only for display and

LEFT: Intricate grass baskets woven by the Papago are displayed at the Indian Summer Pow-wow in Milwaukee, Wisconsin. (*Michael Shedlock/New England Stock Photo*)

OPPOSITE BOTTOM: A very young Zuni boy learns the songs and the dances of his ancestors. Traditions remain particularly strong in the Southwest. (*Kenji Kawano*)

RIGHT: Tiny finger baskets for sale at the huge Santa Fe Indian Market, which draws thousands of visitors from all over the world every summer. (*Brompton Picture Library*)

are not crafted with a utilitarian use in mind. They are intended as works of art.

Ancient painting was not only executed on the walls of pottery vessels but was also done as large murals on kiva walls in the Southwest. As interest in Indian art increases, painting has become increasingly important. More contemporary expression is in watercolor, tempera and acrylic paintings on paper or, occasionally, in oil on canvas. Southwest Indian artists who work in pottery and weaving and other traditional media have not declined so rapidly as the number of painters has increased. Some of the painting is market driven, with Indian artists working in both

Indian and non-Indian motifs. Because of the gallery system, compositions and themes are sometimes determined by not only the artist but also by the patron. Nevertheless, high standards of concept and technique are maintained.

The artistic culture of the Indians of the Southwest is very much alive and well. The culture did not pass with the coming of the great masses of immigrants into the area. Many Indian craftsmen today are creating a wide range of objects for their own use as well as for trade and sale. Huge Indian art fairs are held throughout the country, especially in the Southwest (particularly in Phoenix and Santa Fe), at which Indian artists sell their work to the public.

The art is, and always has been, woven into the fabric of everyday life. It is collected by museums as well as by corporations and individuals. It is appreciated worldwide, as evidenced by the many visitors from other countries who come to the art fairs and markets and visit the museums and galleries that exhibit Indian arts. Indian art forms are appreciated as fine art, rising above their ethnographic and utilitarian aspects.

Over the last half millennium, Indian people have bridged many incursions into their traditional cultures. During this time, subtle changes have occurred in traditional art forms as Indian people encountered new materials and people from other cultures. The Indian artists of the Southwest have been masters at creating designs from a rich variety of forms and materials. Their masterful art forms give distinction and character to the region.

In any society, a healthy balance is achieved through a variety of means, including basic and individual differences. The economic system of a culture, the necessity of making a livelihood, combined with sincere internalized demands for maintenance of tradition and social conformity, brings difficult decisions to the artists. Can Indian art without a basis in tradition be classified as "Indian art?" Is art made by an Indian different from "Indian art?" Such questions are open for discussion. The degree to which Indian artists can select aesthetic criteria from other cultures is a matter of concern that brings with it a dimension of responsibility, because a culture maintains its traditions through its art forms. Does tampering with the art forms cause changes to occur in the traditions?

There is great diversity in American Indian art and its inherent meanings that can be served in any one book even in several volumes. This provides merely an introduction to the art of the Indians of the Southwest. Many of their art forms serve sacred functions and may not be viewed by outsiders. Nevertheless, spirituality cannot help but pervade their more common forms, just as in Western and Eastern societies. After all, art in its original manifestations grew out of human desire to pay homage to unseen spiritual/supernatural forces. Thus, the art of many people today, particularly art of indigenous people, functions to testify how the legends, stories, and religious sensitivities of the cultures were transmitted. The art conventions of the Southwest also serve as messengers of the cultures of which they speak.

THE PLATES

OPPOSITE:
Three Chacoan Bowls
with geometric patterns
Pueblo Bonito, Room 38,
Chaco Canyon, New Mexico
American Museum of Natural
History, New York, NY
Photograph by Craig Chesek

ABOVE:
St. John's Prehistoric
Pottery Bowls
Diameter: 8½ inches
Blitz Antique Native American Art
Ltd, Crompond, NY
Photograph by Charles Bechtold

LEFT:
Corrugated Ware Drinking
Vessels
showing finger daubing technique
of decoration
Chaco Canyon, New Mexico
American Museum of Natural
History, New York, NY
Photograph by P. Hollembeak/J.
Beckett

OPPOSITE:
Drinking Vessels
with geometric patterns
Pueblo Bonito, Room 28,
Chaco Canyon, New Mexico
American Museum of Natural
History, New York, NY
Photograph by P. Hollembeak/J.
Beckett

Anasazi Black-on-White
Olla, c. 950-1100 A.D.
Height: 8½ inches
Blitz Antique Native American Art
Ltd, Crompond, NY
Photograph by Charles Bechtold

RIGHT:
Prehistoric Mimbres Black-on-White Bowl
with three border bands and fish design, hole in center
Purchased from E.D. Osborn, 1919
American Museum of Natural History, New York, NY
Photograph by A. Singer

RIGHT:
Large Red Anasazi Bowl,
c. 100-500 A.D.
Pueblo I, Canyon del Muerto, New Mexico
American Museum of Natural History, New York, NY
Photograph by Dan Coleman

LEFT:
Classic Mimbres Black-on-White Bowl, c. 950-1150 A.D.
This bowl, placed over the head of a deceased member of the tribe, had a hole broken into the center to provide a way for the spirit to depart
Diameter: 13¾ inches
Blitz Antique Native American Art Ltd, Crompond, NY
Photograph by Charles Bechtold

BELOW:
Painted Laguna Jar
with geometric pattern, 1910-1920
Laguna Pueblo, New Mexico
School of American Research, Santa Fe, NM

ABOVE:
Santa Ana Water Jar
with black rim and unusual red
band on interior of mouth, 1925-
1940
Santa Ana Pueblo, New
Mexico
School of American Research, Santa
Fe, NM

ABOVE:
Santo Domingo Water Jar
with concave base, featuring an
eight-panel design, 1930-1940
Santo Domingo Pueblo,
New Mexico
School of American Research, Santa
Fe, NM

RIGHT:
Painted Santo Domingo
Food Bowl
with interior and exterior painted
designs, 1880-1890
Santo Domingo Pueblo,
New Mexico
School of American Research, Santa
Fe, NM

41

ABOVE:
Large Zuni Jar
decorated with deer with
heartlines and various birds
Collected 1899, Zuni
Pueblo, New Mexico
American Museum of Natural
History, New York, NY

OPPOSITE:
Zuni Black-on-White
Ceramic Jar, c. 1880-1890
Zuni Pueblo, New Mexico
Diameter: 12 inches
Christopher Selser, Santa Fe, NM
Photograph by Herb Lotz, Santa Fe,
NM

42

LEFT:
Zuni Water Jar
with running scroll design,
c. 1890-1910
Zuni Pueblo, New Mexico
School of American Research, Santa Fe, NM

LEFT:
Zuni Water Jar
with running scroll design,
c. 1890-1910
Zuni Pueblo, New Mexico
School of American Research, Santa Fe, NM

43

OPPOSITE:
Painted Zia Olla
with floral pattern, c.1895
(showing top and side views)
Zia Pueblo, New Mexico
Charles Donaldson Native American
Art, Scottsdale, AZ
Photograph by Al Costanzo

ABOVE:
Zia Polychrome Storage
Jar "Tinaja," c. 1925
Zia Pueblo, New Mexico
19 × 22 inches
National Museum of the American
Indian, Heye Foundation, New
York, NY
Smithsonian Institution

Acoma Polychrome Jar
Acoma Pueblo, New Mexico
Height: 7 inches
Blitz Antique Native American Art
Ltd, Crompond, NY
Photograph by Charles Bechtold

Acoma Ceramic Jar
with floral pattern and figure of
bird, c. 1890
Acoma Pueblo, New Mexico
Diameter: 11 inches
Christopher Selser, Santa Fe, NM
Photograph by Herb Lotz, Santa Fe,
NM

Acoma Negative Pattern
Olla, c. 1900
Acoma Pueblo, New Mexico
Charles Donaldson Native American
Art, Scottsdale, AZ
Photograph by Al Costanzo

RIGHT:
**Acoma Polychrome
Ceramic Jar**
**with large bird and flowers,
c. 1890**
Acoma Pueblo, New Mexico
Diameter: 12 inches
Christopher Selser, Santa Fe, NM
*Photograph by Herb Lotz, Santa Fe,
NM*

RIGHT:
**Acoma Polychrome
Ceramic Jar, c. 1875**
Acoma Pueblo, New Mexico
Diameter: 12½ inches
Christopher Selser, Santa Fe, NM
*Photograph by Herb Lotz, Santa Fe,
NM*

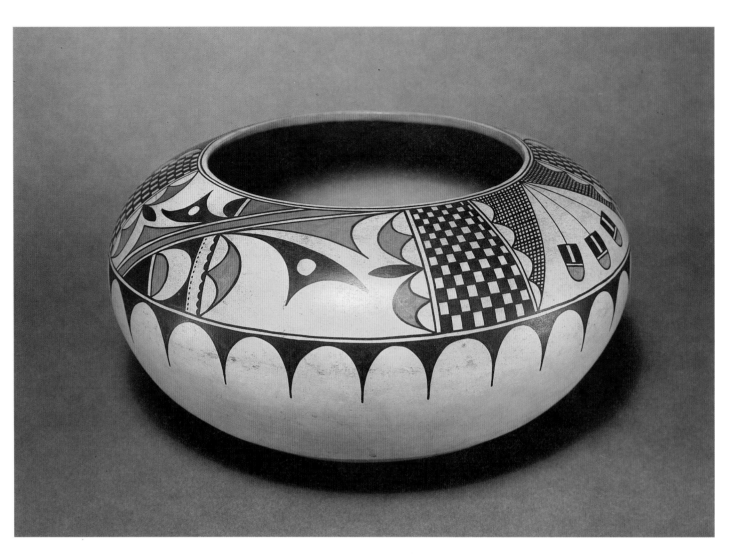

ABOVE:

**San Ildefonso Ceremonial
Pot,** used to store corn in the
kiva for the next season's planting
Made by Maria Martinez,
designed by Julian Martinez,
c. 1910
San Ildefonso Pueblo, New
Mexico
*American Museum of Natural
History, New York, NY*

LEFT:

San Ildefonso Food Bowl,
butterfly design on red-slipped
exterior, 1900-1910
Made by Maria Martinez,
decorated by Julian Martinez
San Ildefonso Pueblo, New
Mexico
*School for American Research, Santa
Fe, NM*

OPPOSITE:

Acoma Polychrome Jar,
1920-1930
Acoma Pueblo, New Mexico
*American Museum of Natural
History, New York, NY*

ABOVE LEFT:
San Ildefonso Water Jar, red-slipped with black painted decoration in a water spider design
Made by Tonita Roybal, 1920-1940
San Ildefonso Pueblo, New Mexico
School of American Research, Santa Fe, NM

LEFT:
San Ildefonso Water Jar, showing an unusual bird with antlers, 1890-1910
San Ildefonso Pueblo, New Mexico
School of American Research, Santa Fe, NM

OPPOSITE:
San Ildefonso Black-on-Black and Buff-on-Sienna Pottery, with Avanyu (plumed serpent) design, c. 1965
Made by Maria and Popovi Da Martinez
San Ildefonso Pueblo, New Mexico
Black-on-black: height: 6 inches; buff-on-sienna: height: 4½ inches
Courtesy Gallery 10, Scottsdale, AZ and Santa Fe, NM

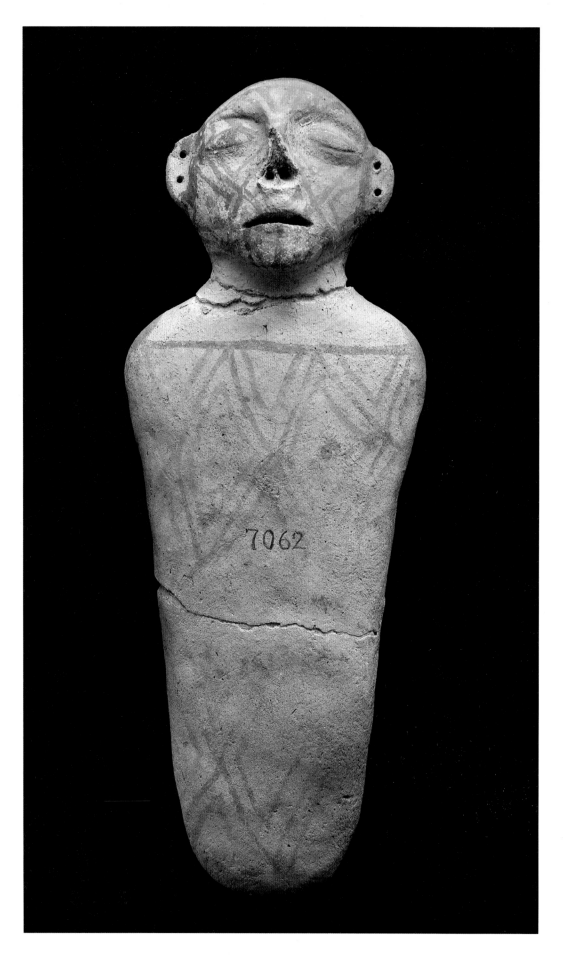

LEFT:
Mohave Doll,
collected 1854
Rio Colorado, California
Painted pottery
Collected by Jules Marcou
Peabody Museum/Harvard
University, Cambridge, MA
Photograph by Hillel Burger

OPPOSITE:
Mohave Doll,
collected c. 1880
Painted pottery with beads
and hair
Gift of Miss Nellie M. Betteley, 1905
Peabody Museum/Harvard
University, Cambridge, MA
Photograph by Hillel Burger

LEFT:
**Hopi Mother and Child
Figure, c. 1890**
Carved and painted wood
Height: 8 inches
Christopher Selser, Santa Fe, NM
Photograph by Herb Lotz, Santa Fe,
NM

OPPOSITE:
**Contemporary Cochiti
Figure, "The Chanter,"
1990s**
**Made by Virgil Ortiz, who is
reviving this type of ceramic
"reportage" art from the early
1900s**
Cochiti Pueblo, New
Mexico
Hollow painted ceramic, pit-
fired in traditional manner
Height: 14 inches
Four Winds Gallery, Pittsburgh, PA
Photograph by Marcy Holquist

TOP LEFT:
Pima Basket,
1890-1910
Southern Arizona
Coiled cattail splints sewn
with willow and martymia
*School of American Research, Santa
Fe, NM*

ABOVE:
Pima Basket,
1900-1920
Southern Arizona
Coil weave with twill weave
in center of base
*School of American Research, Santa
Fe, NM*

LEFT:
Pima Basket,
1900-1920
Southern Arizona
Close coil with birch
foundation
*School of American Research, Santa
Fe, NM*

ABOVE:
Western Apache Basket,
1910-1920
Arizona
Coil weave with animal and
human figures
School of American Research, Santa
Fe, NM

RIGHT:
Western Apache Basket
Arizona
Coil weave with rows of
animal and human figures
School of American Research, Santa
Fe, NM

**Apache and Yavapai
Basket Trays, 1900-1910**
Cottonwood and devil's claw
*Courtesy Morning Star Gallery,
Santa Fe, NM*
Photograph by Addison Doty

OPPOSITE:
Yavapai Basketry Tray
with human and animal figures,
c. 1910
Diameter: 20 inches
Christopher Selser, Santa Fe, NM
Photograph by Herb Lotz, Santa Fe,
NM

ABOVE:
Apache Coiled Tray and
Olla
Tray: diameter: 17 inches;
Olla: height: 14 inches
Blitz Antique Native American Art
Ltd, Crompond, NY
Photograph by Charles Bechtold

OPPOSITE TOP:
**Navajo Second Phase
Chief's Blanket, c. 1860s**
73 × 47 inches
*Christopher Selser, Santa Fe, NM
Photograph by Herb Lotz, Santa Fe,
NM*

OPPOSITE BOTTOM:
**Navajo Late Classic Third
Phase Chief's Blanket,**
c. 1870
55 × 71 inches
Woven of ravelled American
flannel, handspun indigo
blue and natural white
*Courtesy Second Phase Gallery,
Taos, NM*

ABOVE:
Navajo Classic Serape,
c. 1865
74 × 52 inches
*Christopher Selser, Santa Fe, NM
Photograph by Herb Lotz, Santa Fe,
NM*

OPPOSITE:
**Navajo Late Classic
Child's Wearing Blanket,**
c. 1880

44 × 31 inches
*Blitz Antique Native American Art
Ltd, Crompond, NY
Photograph by Charles Bechtold*

RIGHT:
Navajo Child's Serape,
c. 1875

48 × 32 inches
*Christopher Selser, Santa Fe, NM
Photograph by Herb Lotz, NM*

LEFT:
Navajo Moki Serape,
c. 1875
72 × 48 inches
Christopher Selser, Santa Fe, NM
Photograph by Herb Lotz, Santa Fe,
NM

OPPOSITE:
Navajo Germantown
Serape with Moki style design,
c. 1895
53 × 90 inches
Woven of aniline-dyed four-
ply commercial yarn
Courtesy Second Phase Gallery,
Taos, NM

ABOVE:
Late Classic Navajo First Phase Chief's Blanket,
c. 1875-1880
54 × 77 inches
Woven of handspun and ravelled aniline-dyed red yarn with handspun indigo blue and natural handspun brown and white yarn
Courtesy Second Phase Gallery, Taos, NM

OPPOSITE:
Navajo Poncho
Collection of Dr. I. Bittenger
American Museum of Natural History, New York, NY

71

LEFT:
Navajo Classic Period Child's Serape, c. 1860
29 × 52 inches
Woven of cochineal-dyed bayetta with handspun indigo blue and natural green and white yarn
Courtesy Second Phase Gallery, Taos, NM

OPPOSITE:
Navajo Moki Woman's Wearing Blanket, c. 1875
Charles Donaldson Native American Art, Scottsdale, AZ
Photograph by Al Costanzo

ABOVE:
Hopi Kachina Manta
*American Museum of Natural
History, New York, NY
Photograph by Kerry Perkins*

OPPOSITE:
**Navajo Textile – Teec Nos
Pos Style,** c. 1993
Made by Marian Nez
88 × 111 inches
Commercial wool
*Courtesy of the Santa Fe Collection
and Cristof's, Santa Fe, NM*

**Navajo Transitional
Eyedazzler** with cowboy
pictorial center, c. 1890-1895
53 × 77 inches
Woven of handspun yarns
with aniline and natural dyes
*Courtesy Second Phase Gallery,
Taos, NM*

Navajo Saltillo-Style
Germantown Eyedazzler
Includes pictorial imagery, rare
for this type of weaving, 1885-1895
30½ × 63 inches
Collection of America Hurrah, New
York, NY

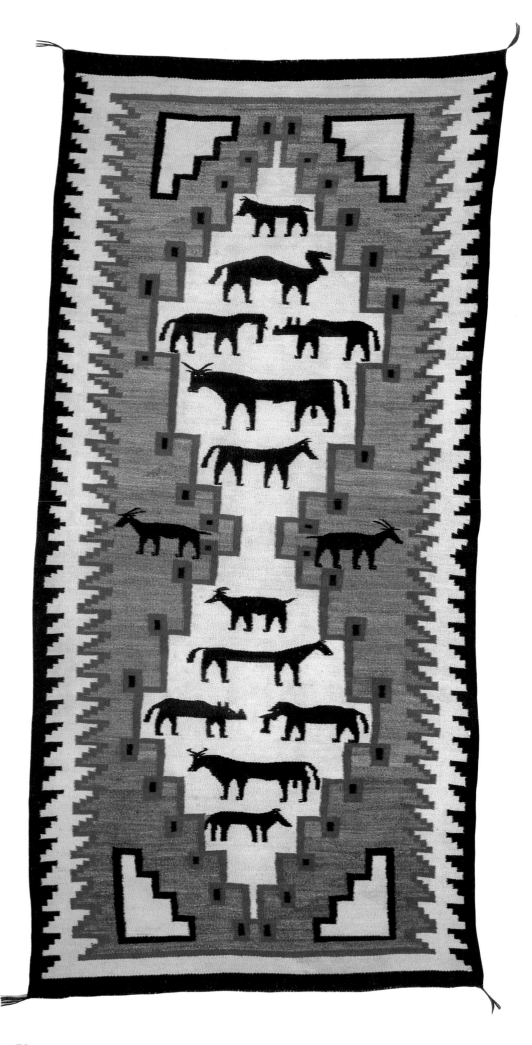

LEFT:
Navajo Weaving
featuring various animals
51 × 103 inches
Collection of America Hurrah, New York, NY

OPPOSITE:
Navajo Germantown Serape, with images of cowboys, 1875-1885
51 × 81 inches
Private Collection
Photograph courtesy Sotheby's, Inc, New York, NY

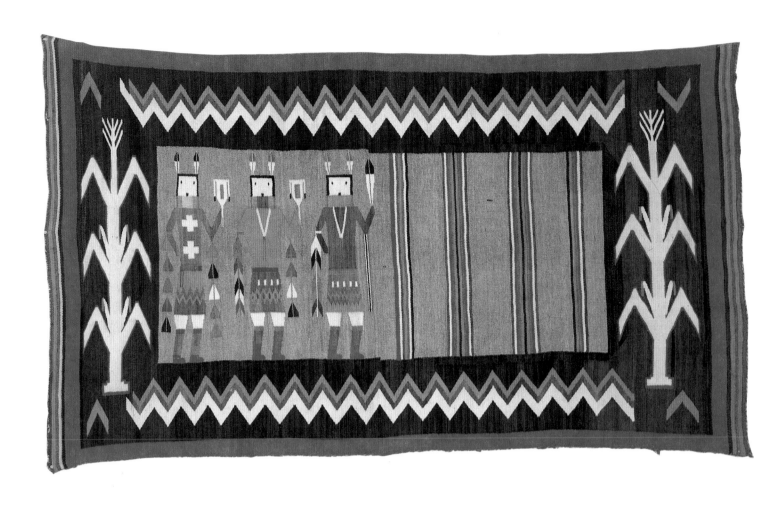

ABOVE:
Navajo Handspun Yei Rug
with three female Yei figures and
rainbow-like striped bars, flanked
by sacred corn plants, c. 1920
76 × 42 inches
*Collection of America Hurrah, New
York, NY*

OPPOSITE:
Navajo Handspun Blanket
with a herd of cattle and long-
legged birds that might be
roadrunners, c. 1890
50 × 71 inches
*Collection of America Hurrah, New
York, NY*

81

Navajo Weaving, "Corn Stalks on a Mesa,"
late 1920s
Natural homespun yarns, showing an eccentric weave for the corn tassels
The Halpern Collection
Courtesy J. Mark Sublette/Medicine Man Gallery, Tucson, AZ
Photograph by Robin Stancliff

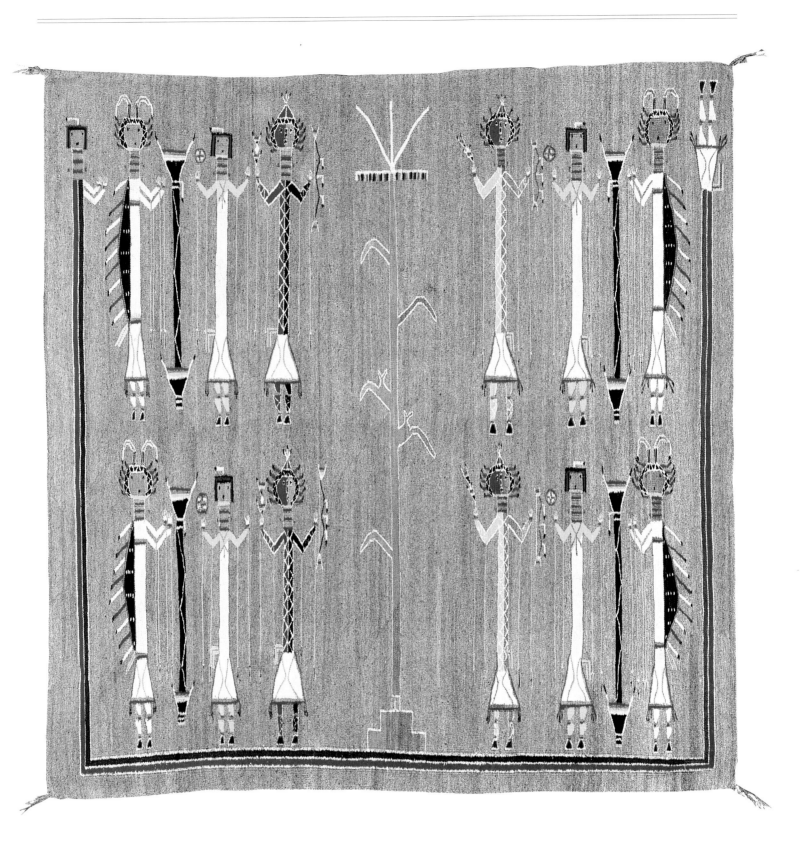

Navajo Rug
depicting a sandpainting from the
Nightway Chant, c. 1930
Woven by Gladys Manuelito, a
niece of Hosteen Klah, who was
the first weaver to show
sandpaintings in his work
68 × 68 inches
*Courtesy Second Phase Gallery,
Taos, NM*

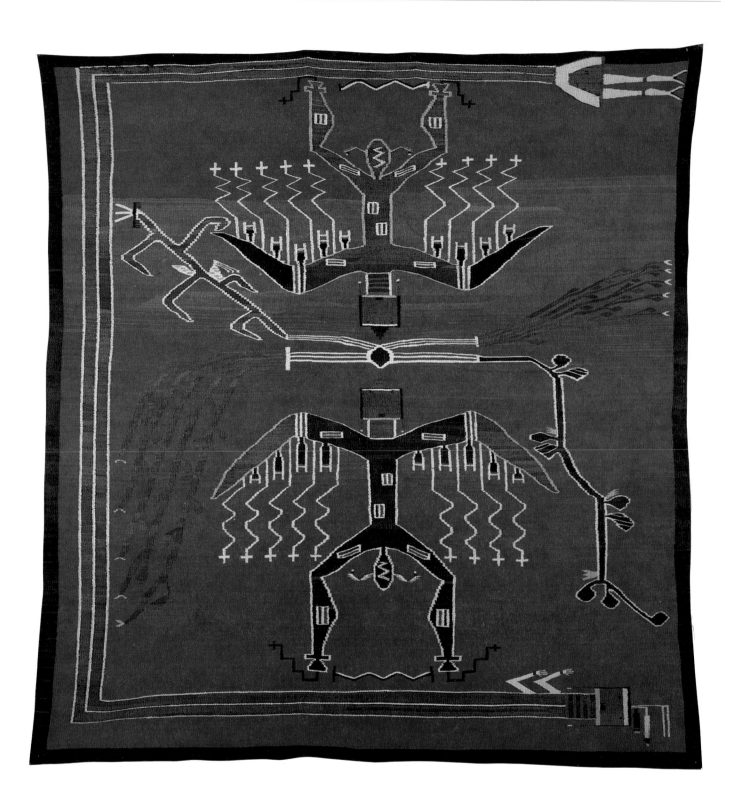

ABOVE:

Navajo Weaving, 1925-1930, shows sandpainting variation, using only two of the four Summer Thunders (Black Thunder in the East and Blue Thunder in the West) that are normally shown in **The Summer Thunder with Sacred Plants Sandpainting** done in conjunction with the Male Shootingway Chant. Male lightning bolts and rain are shown and the plants are beans, tobacco, corn and squash. The Rainbow Guardian, not normally part of this sandpainting, has been added for design effect

70 × 75 inches

Collection of America Hurrah, New York, NY

OPPOSITE:

Navajo Germantown Weaving on loom, showing four-star flag, rare for this period, c. 1885

17 × 19 inches

Collection of America Hurrah, New York, NY

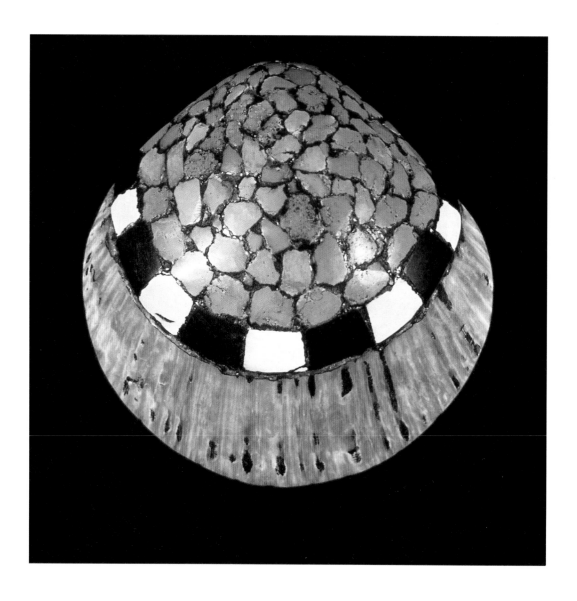

ABOVE:
Zuni Shell Pendant
Zuni Pueblo, New Mexico
Spiny oyster with white shell
and jet
*School of American Research, Santa
Fe, NM*

OPPOSITE:
**Zuni Knife Wing Inlay
Pins, c. 1930**
Silver, turquoise, jet, coral,
abalone
*Four Winds Gallery, Pittsburgh, PA
Photograph by Marcy Holquist*

86

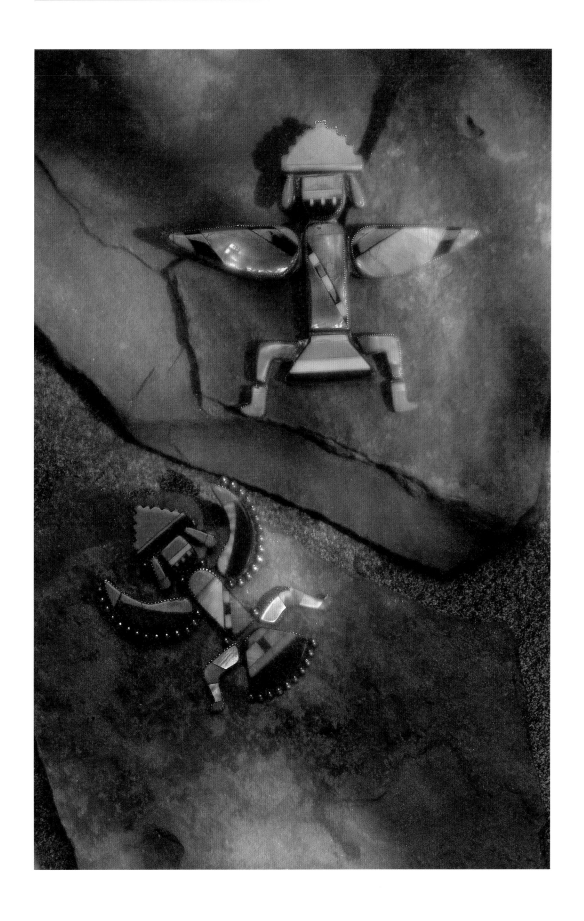

LEFT:
Hopi Bracelet
Coral, turquoise and silver
School of American Research, Santa Fe, NM

BELOW LEFT:
Hopi Pin
Silver with turquoise inset
School of American Research, Santa Fe, NM

RIGHT:
Zuni Butterfly Pin,
"Old Pawn," pre-1950
Hand-stamped sterling silver
Collection of Rowena Martinez,
El Rincon, Taos, NM
Photograph by Gail Russell

BELOW RIGHT:
Zuni Bracelet,
"Old Pawn," pre-1950
Silver, turquoise, coral,
mother-of-pearl, jet
Collection of Rowena Martinez,
El Rincon, Taos, NM
Photograph by Gail Russell

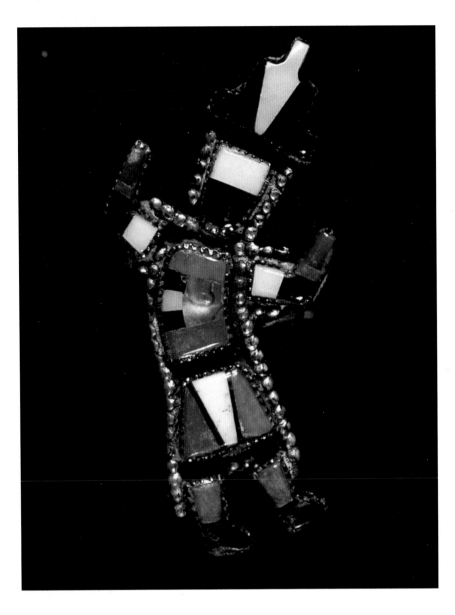

LEFT:
Zuni Ring,
with rainbow man design
Silver, coral, jet, turquoise
School of American Research, Santa Fe, NM

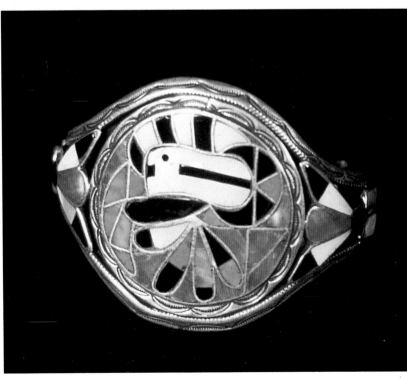

LEFT:
Zuni Bracelet
Silver, spiny oyster, mother-of-pearl
School of American Research, Santa Fe, NM

RIGHT:
(From top):
Navajo Bracelet,
c. 1940
Sterling silver with turquoise,
twisted wire
Navajo Bracelet,
c. 1940
Hand-stamped sterling silver with
turquoise
Navajo Bracelet,
c. 1940
Sterling silver with turquoise,
twisted wire, solder balls
Navajo Bracelet,
c. 1930
Hand-stamped sterling silver
Navajo Bracelet,
c. 1930
Sterling silver with turquoise,
twisted wire, solder balls
Navajo Bracelet,
c. 1930
Sterling silver with turquoise,
twisted wire, solder balls
Navajo Bracelet,
c. 1930
Sterling silver with turquoise,
twisted wire
Haida (Northwest Coast) Bracelet,
c. 1910
Hand-stamped ingot silver
Navajo Bracelet,
c. 1940
Sterling silver with turquoise,
twisted wire, stamped solder balls
Navajo Bracelet,
c. 1940
Sterling silver with turquoise,
twisted wire, solder balls
Navajo Bracelet,
c. 1940
Hand-stamped sterling silver with
turquoise, solder balls
Navajo Bracelet,
c. 1940
Hand-stamped sterling silver with
turquoise, twisted wire
Zuni Bracelet,
c. 1940
Sterling silver with petit point
turquoise, solder balls, twisted wire
Navajo Bracelet,
c. 1930
Hand-stamped sterling silver with
turquoise, twisted wire
Navajo Bracelet,
c. 1940
Hand-stamped sterling silver with
turquoise, twisted wire, solder balls
Courtesy Morning Star Gallery, Santa Fe,
New Mexico
Photograph by Addison Doty

LEFT:
Navajo Earrings
with eagle claw design
Silver and turquoise insets
School of American Research, Santa Fe, NM

OPPOSITE:
Navajo Ketoh (Bow Guard)
Cast silver with turquoise inset
School of American Research, Santa Fe, NM

OPPOSITE:
Navajo Buckle
with stamped rosettes and appliquéd leaf
Silver with insets of turquoise and coral
School of American Research, Santa Fe, NM

LEFT:
Contemporary Hopi Bracelet, 1990s
with rainbow/cornplant design
Made by Bernard Dawahoya
School of American Research, Santa Fe, NM

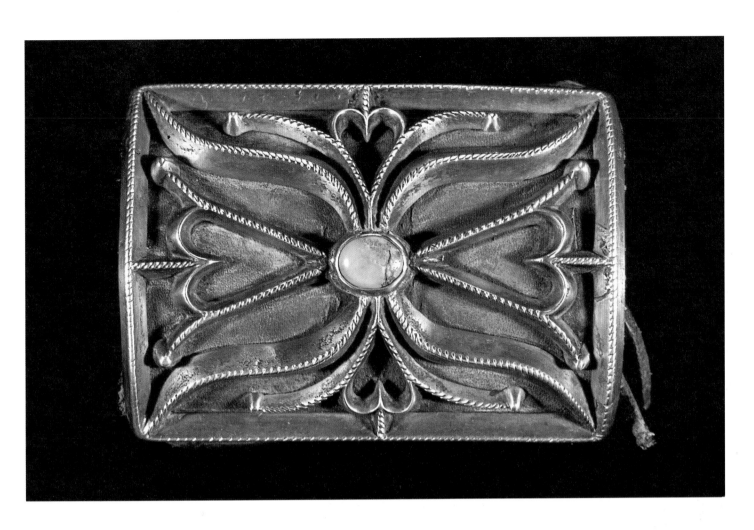

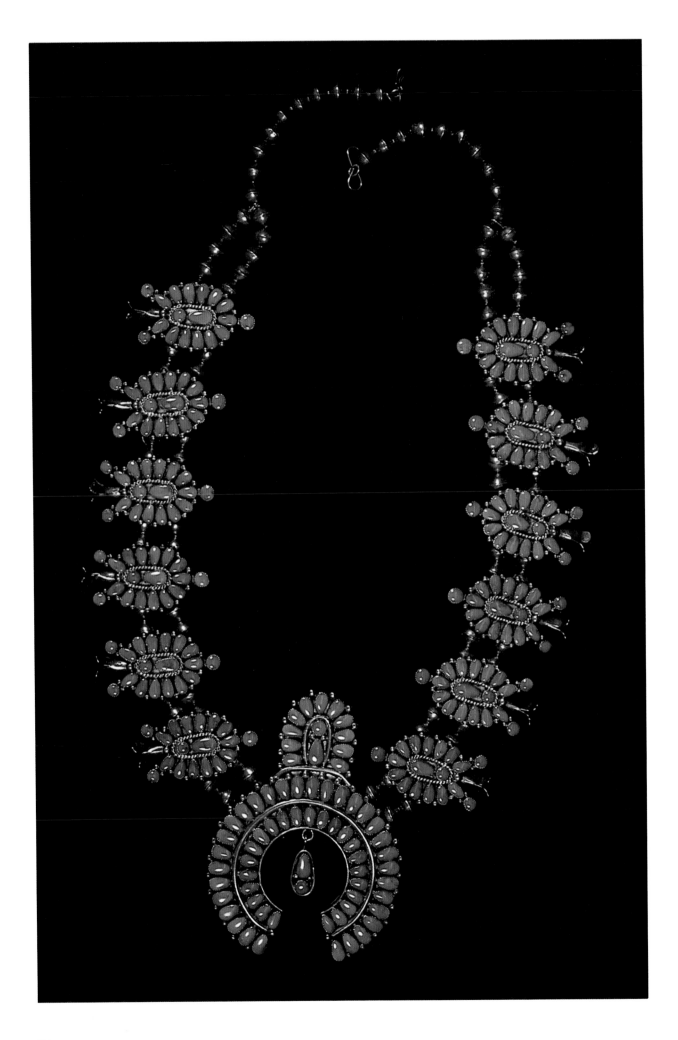

**Zuni Squash Blossom
Necklace,** c. 1940
Turquoise, silver,
commercial stringing wire
*San Diego Museum of Man, San
Diego, CA*
Photograph by Ken Hedges

ABOVE:
Zuni Necklace
Abalone, white mussel shell,
jet, coral
*School of American Research, Santa
Fe, NM*

ABOVE:
Navajo Necklace
with eagle claw design
Silver with turquoise insets
School of American Research, Santa
Fe, NM

ABOVE:
Hopi Necklace (Choker)
Silver with turquoise insets
School of American Research, Santa
Fe, NM

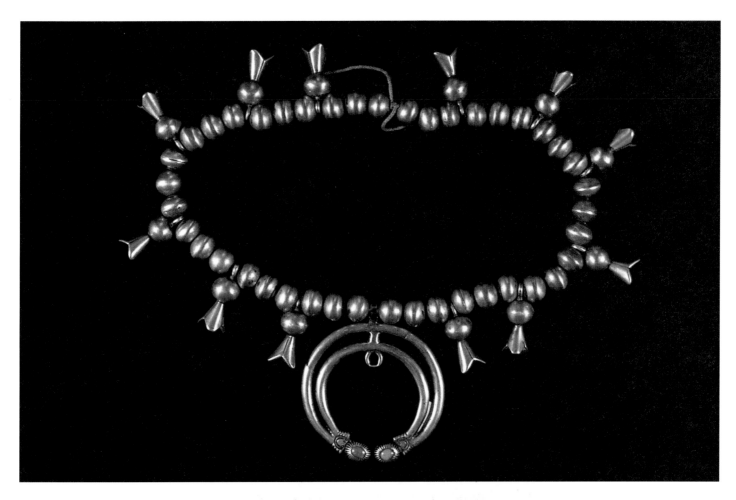

ABOVE:
**Navajo Squash Blossom
Necklace**
Silver with turquoise insets
*School of American Research, Santa
Fe, NM*

LEFT:
Navajo Necklace
Silver with blue turquoise
*School of American Research, Santa
Fe, NM*

LEFT:
Santo Domingo Necklace
Santo Domingo Pueblo,
New Mexico
White shell discs, spiny
oyster
*School of American Research, Santa
Fe, NM*

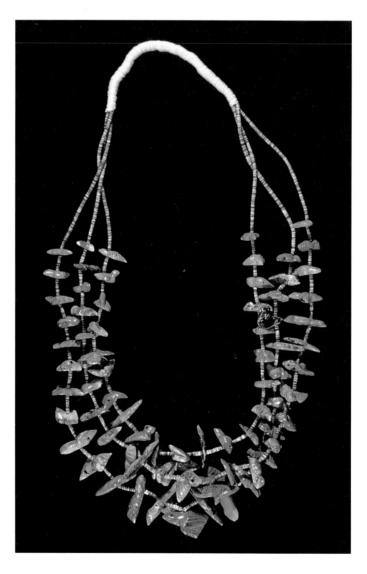

RIGHT:
Zuni Fetish Necklace
strung with olive shells and
turquoise
*School of American Research, Santa
Fe, NM*

RIGHT:
Zuni Fetish Necklace
*School of American Research, Santa
Fe, NM*

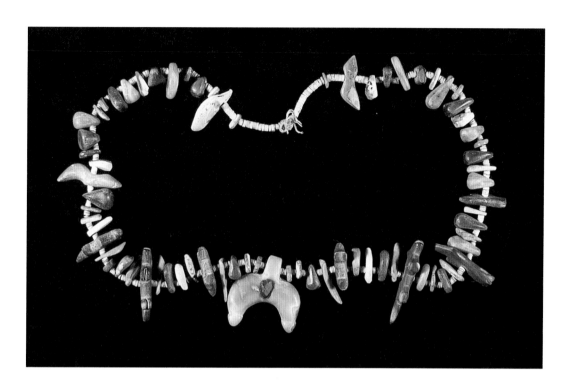

LEFT:
Zuni Bird Fetish Necklace
*School of American Research, Santa
Fe, NM*

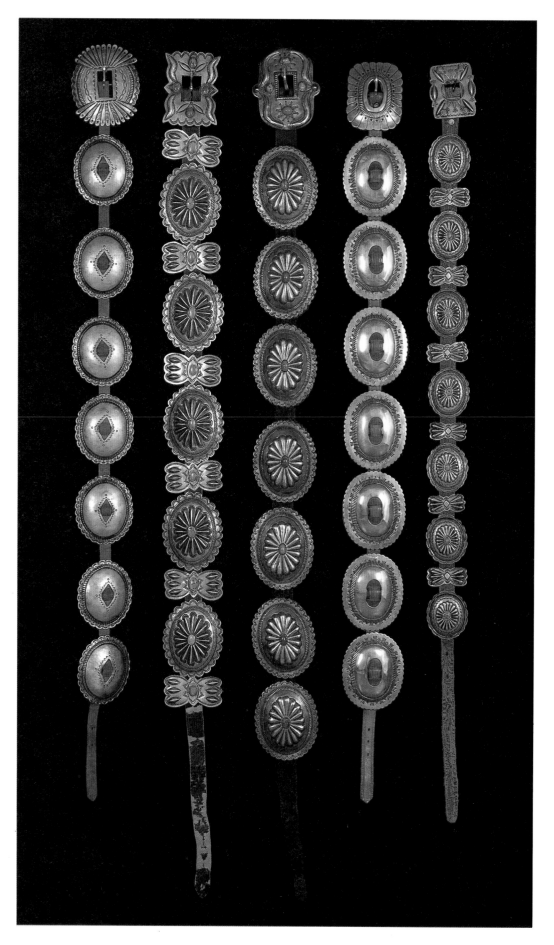

(Left to right):
Navajo Revival Concha Belt, c. 1930
Stamped diamond-slot sterling silver, leather strap
Conchas 3½ inches diameter
Navajo Concha Belt, c. 1930
Stamped silver ornamented with hand-stamping, repoussé, turquoise and butterfly-shaped conchas, leather strap
Conchas 4 inches diameter
Navajo Concha Belt, c. 1920
Sterling silver with hand stamping, repoussé, turquoise, leather strap
Conchas 4 inches diameter
Navajo Concha Belt, c. 1940
Ambrose Roanhorse
Sterling silver, leather strap
Conchas 4 inches diameter
Navajo Concha Belt, c. 1920
Sterling silver ornamented with hand stamping, repoussé, turquoise, leather strap
Conchas 2½ inches diameter
Courtesy Morning Star Gallery, Santa Fe, New Mexico
Photograph by Addison Doty

Apache Saddle Bag
with geometric design
Buckskin with rawhide
fringe and cloth
Peabody Essex Museum, Salem, MA
Photograph by Mark Sexton

**Pair of Pueblo Cradle
Boards and Double Board
Navajo Cradle Board,**
19th century
*Blitz Antique Native American Art
Ltd, Crompond, NY*
Photograph by Charles Bechtold

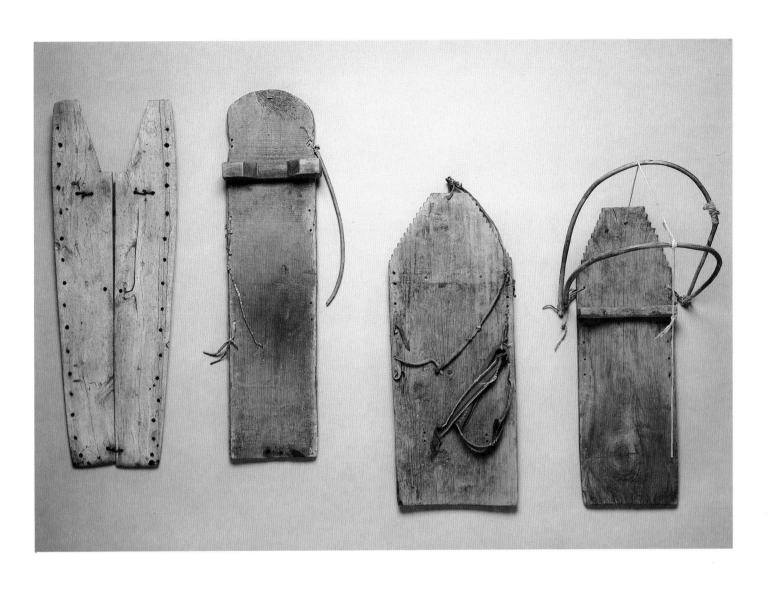

**Navajo Double Cradle
Board and Three Pueblo
Cradle Boards,**
19th century
*Blitz Antique Native American Art
Ltd, Crompond, NY*
Photograph by Charles Bechtold

103

Apache Cradle Board,
late 19th century
Wood and canvas
Length: 42 inches
Blitz Antique Native American Art
Ltd, Crompond, NY
Photograph by Charles Bechtold

Navajo Cradle Board
Length: 45 inches
*Blitz Antique Native American Art
Ltd, Crompond, NY
Photograph by Charles Bechtold*

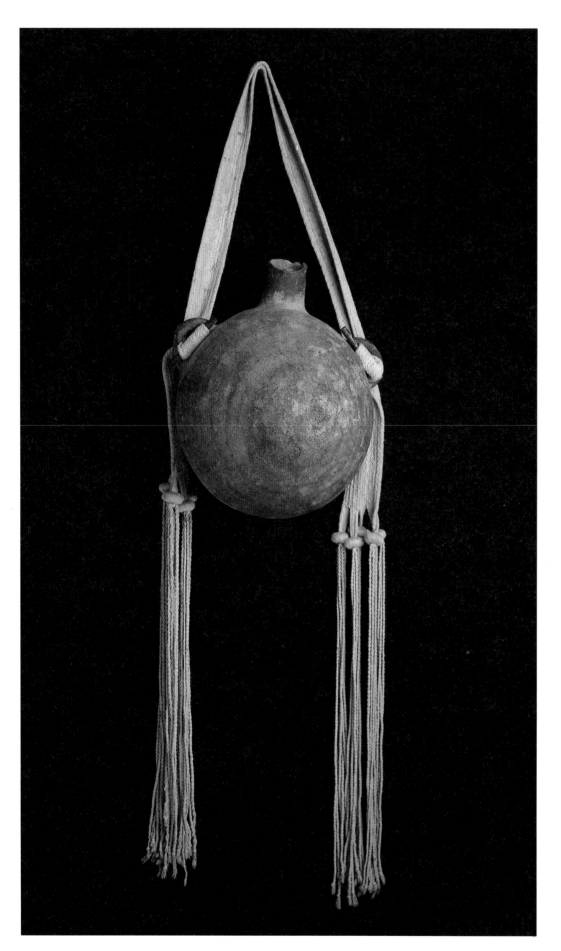

LEFT:
Hopi Pottery Canteen and Rain Sash, mid-19th century
Diameter: 34 inches; height: 14 inches
Blitz Antique Native American Art Ltd, Crompond, NY
Photograph by Charles Bechtold

OPPOSITE:
Two Zuni Pottery Canteens with Pueblo Sashes, c. 1880
Height: 9½ inches
Originally in Smithsonian Institution Collections
Blitz Antique Native American Art Ltd, Crompond, NY
Photograph by Charles Bechtold

RIGHT:

Hopi Sun Design Dance Shield
showing corn stalks on the front and sunflower design on the back, 1949
Made by Tewaquaptewa of Old Oraibi
San Diego Museum of Man, San Diego, CA
Photograph by Linda Fisk

BELOW:

Navajo Shield
with bow and arrow and deer design within crescent
Made by Many Horses, as replica of his own shield
Diameter: 24 inches
Painted hide with feathers and cloth
Collected by J.M. Johnson
Cranbrook Institute of Science, Bloomfield Hills, MI

OPPOSITE:

Rio Grande Pueblo Shield
with geometric design, c. 1850
Painted hide
Diameter: 19 inches
Christopher Selser, Santa Fe, NM
Photograph by Herb Lotz, Santa Fe, NM

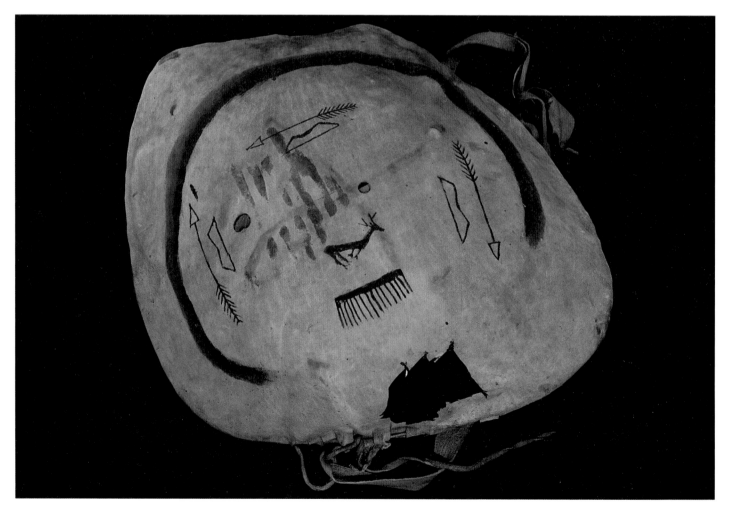

Zuni Pueblo Fetish Jar,
c. 1880s
Diameter: 12½ inches
Christopher Selser, Santa Fe, NM
Photograph by Herb Lotz, Santa Fe,
NM

ABOVE:

Contemporary Fetish
with unusual double figures
Made by Salvador Romero,
Cochiti Pueblo
Carved local stone,
gemstones, turquoise, glass
beads, attached with sinew
San Diego Museum of Man, San
Diego, CA
Photograph by Ken Hedges

BELOW:

Group of Four Fetishes
including a mountain lion (Zuni:
White Mountain Lion of the
East), a wildcat (Zuni: Hunter
God of the South), a coyote
(Zuni: Hunter God of the West)
and an unidentified white animal
(Santo Domingo)
Materials include bone,
sandstone, turquoise, stone,
shell beads, and sinew
San Diego Museum of Man, San
Diego, CA
Photograph by Ken Hedges

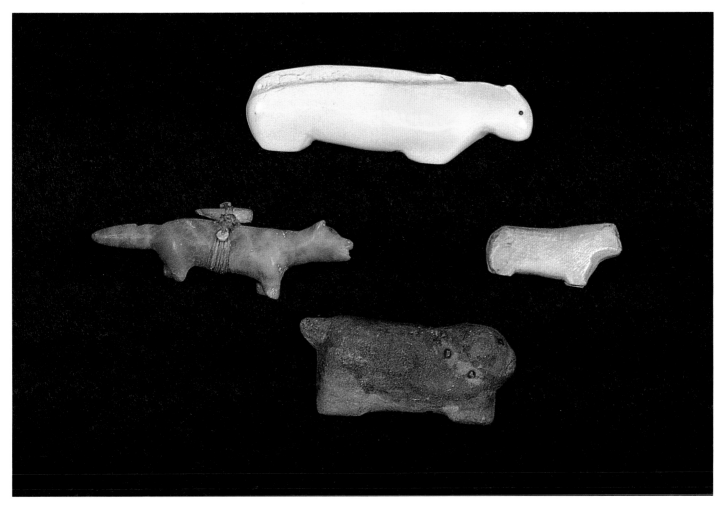

Stone Idol,
prehistoric period
San Lazaro, New Mexico
Excavated by N. C. Nelson in 1912
American Museum of Natural
History, New York, NY
Photograph by J. Beckett

Zuni Mountain Lion Fetish, c. 19th century
Length: 8½ inches
Christopher Selser, Santa Fe, NM
Photograph by Herb Lotz, Santa Fe,
NM

113

Jemez Tablita, c. 1900
Milled lumber, paint
Courtesy Morning Star Gallery, Santa Fe, NM
Photograph by Addison Doty

Jemez Tablita, c. 1860
Cottonwood, cotton trade cloth,
mineral pigment, cotton thread
Courtesy Morning Star Gallery, Santa Fe, NM
Photograph by Addison Doty

LEFT:

Hopi Shalako Mana Kachina Doll, c. 1880
Height: 17 inches
Christopher Selser, Santa Fe, NM
Photograph by Herb Lotz, Santa Fe, NM

OPPOSITE:

Hopi Pahlik Mana (Butterfly Maiden) Kachina Doll, c. 1895
Carved wood, paint, feathers
Charles Donaldson Native American Art, Scottsdale, AZ
Photograph by Al Costanzo

RIGHT:
Zuni Oaku (Kachina Baby Doll), c. 1895
This kachina doll was carried and cared for by a woman wishing to become pregnant, so that the spirits could see that she would make a good mother
Charles Donaldson Native American Art, Scottsdale, AZ
Photograph by Al Costanzo

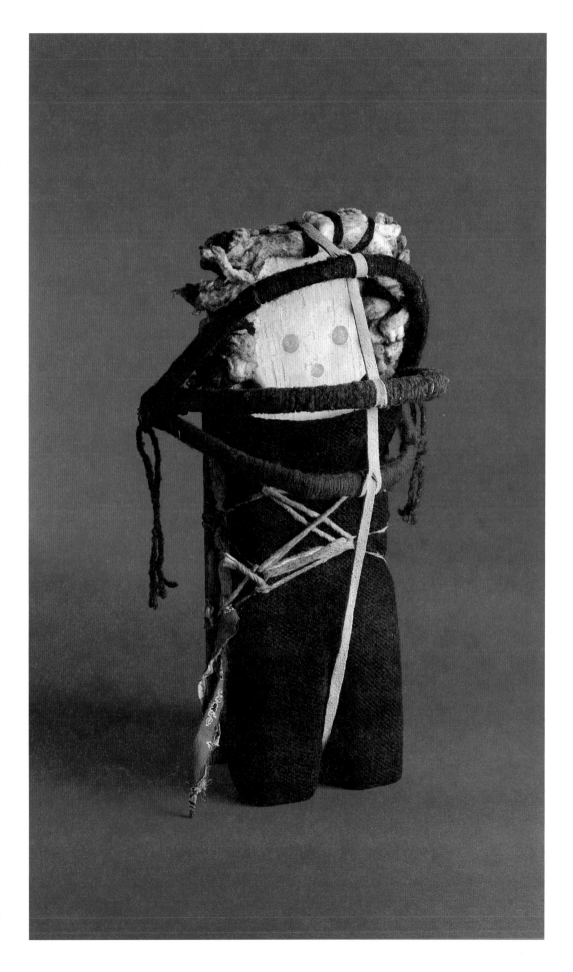

OPPOSITE:
Hopi Kachina Doll of a Comanche Maiden, c. 1920
Charles Donaldson Native American Art, Scottsdale, AZ
Photograph by Al Costanzo

LEFT:
Hopi Buffalo Kachina Doll, c. 1920
Charles Donaldson Native American Art, Scottsdale, AZ
Photograph by Al Costanzo

OPPOSITE:
Hopi Ogre Kachina Doll (Nata-aska), 1966
Made by Jim Kewanwytewa on Hopi Reservation, Oraibi, Arizona
Hand-carved glued and painted wood, leather, feathers, string, fur
Given by Ethel Porter Johnson to the Dr. E.H. Redelings Memorial Collection
San Diego Museum of Man, San Diego, CA

Hopi Kachina Doll (Owaq, or Coal), 1989
Made by Manfred Susunkewa, Spider Clan, Second Mesa, Arizona
Hand-carved and painted from one piece of cottonwood root, with poultry feathers, corn husk, cotton thread
Gift of Ida K. Rigby
San Diego Museum of Man, San Diego, CA

**Hopi Buffalo Kachina Doll
(Mosairu)**
**Made by Otto Pentewa at Old
Oraibi, Arizona**
Hand-carved from water-
worn cottonwood root,
painted, cotton cloth,
feathers
Gift of Mrs. Frank Doran
*San Diego Museum of Man, San
Diego, CA*

Group of Hopi Kachina Dolls, c. 1890-1910
Carved and painted wood
Christopher Selser, Santa Fe, NM
Photograph by Herb Lotz, Santa Fe, NM

124

Three Hopi Kachina Dolls
(Cow, c. 1925; Pahlik Mana
(Butterfly Maiden), c. 1900;
Maiden, c. 1915)
Carved and painted wood
Charles Donaldson Native American
Art, Scottsdale, AZ
Photograph by Al Costanzo

Hopi Kachina Doll (Hilili), c. 1940
Carved wood, feathers, natural earth pigment
Height: 17 inches
San Diego Museum of Man, San Diego, CA
Photograph by Ken Hedges

Hopi Kachina Doll (Hehea's Uncle), 1971
Made by James Kootshongsie, Third Mesa, Arizona
Carved wood, feathers, natural earth pigments
Height: 13 inches
San Diego Museum of Man, San Diego, CA
Photograph by Ken Hedges

BELOW:
Group of Hopi Kachina Dolls, c. 1890-1910
Christopher Selser, Santa Fe, NM
Photograph by Herb Lotz, Santa Fe, NM

PAGE 128:
Navajo Yebichai Rug, c. 1920s
70 × 40 inches
Collection of America Hurrah, New York, NY

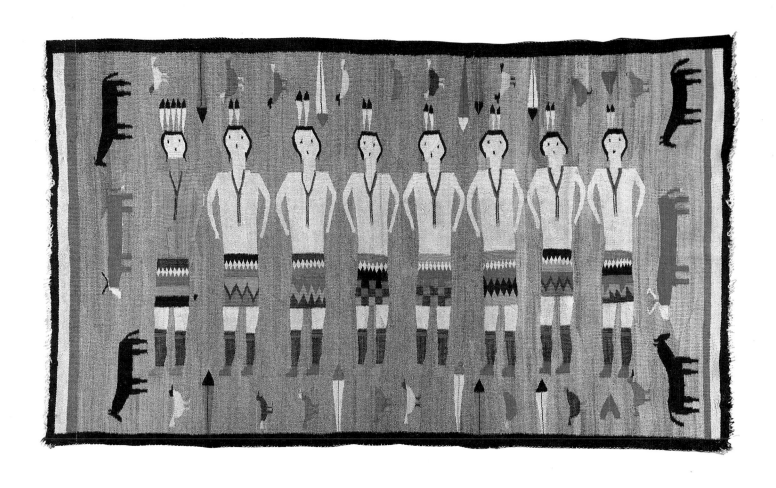

ACKNOWLEDGMENTS

The editors would like to thank the following for their invaluable assistance in the compilation of the images in this book: Joel Sweimler, Special Collections Manager, Department of Library Services, American Museum of Natural History, New York, NY: George Blitz of Blitz Antique Native American Arts Ltd, Crompond, NY and photographer Charles Bechtold; Charles and Leslie Donaldson of Charles Donaldson Native American Arts, Scottsdale, AZ and photographer Al Costanzo; Christopher Selser, Santa Fe, NM and photographer Herb Lotz, Santa Fe, NM; Christy Hoffman and Mike Larking of the School of American Research, Santa Fe, NM; Kenji Kawano, Altus, OK; Betty Johansen, New England Stock Photo, Old Saybrook, CT; Steve Powell and Second Phase Gallery, Taos, NM; Kathy Flynn of the Peabody Essex Museum, Salem, MA and photographer Mark Sexton; Martha Labell, Photographic Archives, Peabody Museum of Archaeology and Ethnology/Harvard University, Cambridge, MA and photographer Hillel Burger; Joel Kopp of America Hurrah, New York, NY; John Krena and Jody Vignale of Four Winds Gallery, Pittsburgh, PA and photographer Marcy Holquist; Morning Star Gallery, Santa Fe, NM; Addison Doty, Santa Fe, NM; Carol DeFord, Collections Department, Cranbrook Institute of Science, Bloomfield Hills, MI; the Halpern Collection; J. Mark Sublette and Amy Steeby of Medicine Man Gallery, Tucson, AZ and photographer Robin Stancliff; Gail Russell, Taos, NM; Rowena Martinez, El Rincon, Taos, NM; Laura McMurchie, Arizona Office of Tourism, Phoenix, AZ; Christof's, Santa Fe, NM and photographer Mark Nohl; Gallery 10, Scottsdale, AZ and Santa Fe, NM; Sotheby's, New York, NY; and the National Museum of the American Indian, Heye Foundation, New York, NY.

The publisher would also like to thank the following individuals who helped in the preparation of this book: Ron Callow and Alan Gooch of Design 23, the designers; Jean Martin, the editor; and Rita Longabucco, the photo editor.